GEORGE WASHINGTON
THE MASON

Wallace McCammant

ISBN 0-7661-0259-9

GEORGE WASHINGTON, THE MASON

By WALLACE McCAMMANT 33°

Master of Research Lodge of Oregon, U. D.*

FREDERICKSBURG Lodge, now known as Fredericksburg Lodge No. 4, operating under the authority of the Grand Lodge of Virginia, is one of the oldest lodges which has functioned continuously in the country. Its first meeting of which we have any record was held on September 1, 1752. We do not know under what authority this meeting was held. There may have been in existence some warrant which has since been lost or the brethren may have met pursuant to immemorial usage. The lodge received a charter from the Grand Lodge of Scotland on the 21st of July, 1758.

Masonry at that time was in a formative state, especially in the American colonies. The Grand Lodge of England had been organized only thirty-five years at the time when Fredericksburg Lodge held its first meeting. The first American lodges of whose organization we have satisfactory information were a lodge in Pennsylvania organized in 1730 and a lodge in Massachusetts organized in 1733. The earliest lodge operating in Virginia seems to have been the Norfolk Lodge, but the Fredericksburg Lodge began its work a short time later.

George Washington was initiated as an Entered Apprentice in Fredericksburg Lodge on the 4th of November, 1752. The records of the Lodge are still in existence. They show that he paid an initiation

---

*Address delivered at institution of Research Lodge January 22, 1932.

fee of two pounds three shillings. He was passed to the degree of Fellowcraft on the 3rd of March, 1753, and raised as a Master Mason on the 4th of August, 1753, all in Fredericksburg Lodge. It will be noted that he was initiated just sixty-four days after the first meeting held by the lodge. The records show that Charles Lewis affiliated with Fredericksburg Lodge on the 4th of November, 1752, and paid an affiliation fee of one pound one shilling six pence. Charles Lewis was the brother of Col. Fielding Lewis who married Washington's only sister.

The records of Fredericksburg Lodge did not always disclose the brethren who were present at its meetings. The records do disclose that George Washington was present on September 1, 1753, and January 4, 1755.

When Washington was seven years old his family moved to the Ferry Farm on the Rappahannock opposite Fredericksburg. In 1743 when Washington was eleven years old his father died and Washington became the owner under his father's will of the Ferry Farm. It is doubtful if Washington can be said to have established a home elsewhere until 1759 when he married Martha Dandridge Custis and took up his residence with her at Mount Vernon.

As bearing on the frequency with which Washington attended the meetings of Fredericksburg Lodge it is well to bear in mind the familiar facts with reference to his public service from and after the time when he became a Master Mason. Less than ninety days after that time he set out on a long journey to northwestern Pennsylvania for the purpose of warning the Commander of a French fort that the Frenchman was encroaching on British territory. This journey was taken under instruction from the Governor of Virginia, and the warning carried was a written document signed by Governor Dinwiddie. This incident had much to do with bringing about the clash between France and Great Britain, which we now call the French and Indian

War. Washington was sent to the frontier in the spring of 1754 and became the Commander of the Virginia forces which fought with French troops at Great Meadows in July of that year. In 1755 Washington was with the ill fated expedition of General Edward Braddock.

On his return from that expedition he reported at Boston to Governor Shirley who held supreme military command in the colonies. Under Shirley's instructions Washington defended the frontiers of Virginia which were harassed by hostile Indians. This service continued until the war in America ended in 1759 with the fall of Quebec. It will be noted that Washington's public services were so important and so continuous that even if he can be said to have lived at Fredericksburg from 1753 to 1759 he had little opportunity to attend the meetings of Fredericksburg Lodge.

From and after 1759 Washington lived at Mount Vernon which is distant about forty-five miles from Fredericksburg. The roads were poor and the journey could not be made frequently, especially by a busy man. It is probable that there was no considerable period during which Washington was a regular attendant at the meetings of his mother lodge. He remained a member of this lodge however in good standing until the end of his life.

The Bible on which Washington was obligated is still in the possession of Fredericksburg Lodge. It is a Bible nine inches in length, seven inches in width and an inch and a quarter thick. It was printed at Cambridge, England, in 1668.

In 1782 while Washington was with the army proceedings were taken for the organization of a lodge at Alexandria. A charter was granted by the Grand Lodge of Pennsylvania on the 3rd of February, 1783. Under this charter the Alexandria Lodge was designated as Lodge No. 39.

The Grand Lodge of Virginia was organized in 1778. It granted a charter to Alexandria Lodge under date of April 28, 1788. Under this charter the lodge was designated as Lodge No. 22. It will be noted therefore that the Alexandria Lodge is referred to in the Washington correspondence whenever there is any mention either of Lodge No. 22 or Lodge No. 39. On the 24th of June, 1784, Washington became an honorary member of Alexandria Lodge. The record is still in existence and is as follows:

> "The Worshipful Master with unanimous consent of the brethren was pleased to admit His Excellency General Washington as an honorary member of the Lodge No. 39."

When proceedings were taken to secure for the Alexandria Lodge a charter under the authority of the Grand Lodge of Virginia, Washington became Charter Master. This was in 1788. He was re-elected Master of Alexandria Lodge on the 20th of December, 1788, for the year beginning December 27, 1788. He was therefore Master of Alexandria Lodge No. 22 operating under the authority of the Grand Lodge of Virginia at the time when he was inaugurated President of the United States. Eleven Masons have served this country as its chief magistrate, but Washington was the only one of them who was Master of his Lodge at the time when he became President.

The meeting place of Alexandria Lodge was easily accessible from Mount Vernon and Washington's Masonic activities were more closely connected with it than with his mother lodge at Fredericksburg. It will be noted that under the Masonic law of Washington's time and particularly in the jurisdiction of Virginia dual membership was permitted. As you are all aware the same regulation now obtains in the jurisdiction of Oregon.

The statement is sometimes made that Washington was Grand Master in the jurisdiction of Virginia. This statement is untrue, although the facts give some color to the report.

First steps were taken on the 6th of May, 1777, to organize the Grand Lodge of Virginia. Representatives of five lodges met in convention at Williamsburg on the 23rd of June, 1777. Less than a majority of the Lodges functioning in the State of Virginia being represented, it was deemed improper to do more than communicate with all of the lodges. The communication so issued suggested the election of Washington as Grand Master in the jurisdiction of Virginia. When Washington was advised of the communication which had been so sent out he declined the honor suggested on the ground that he had not been Master of his lodge and also on the ground that his military duties precluded the performance of the duties reasonably to be expected from him if he were to become the Grand Master of his state.

On the 12th of February, 1785, Washington attended a Masonic funeral, presumably conducted by Alexandria Lodge. There is an entry in his diary under the above date as follows:

"Received an Invitation to the Funeral of Willm Ramsay Esqr of Alexandria—the oldest inhabitant of the Town; & went up—walked in procession as a free mason—Mr. Ramsay in his lifetime being one & now buried with the ceremonies & honors due to one."

There are definite Masonic records showing that Washington marched in a Masonic procession in Philadelphia at the St. Johns Day celebration on the 28th of December, 1778; also that he visited American Union Lodge at West Point, New York, on the 24th day of June, 1779, and again on the 27th day of December, 1779, the latter meeting of the lodge being held in Morristown, New Jersey. The records also show that he visited West Point Lodge at West Point on the 24th of June, 1782.

The records of Solomon's Lodge No. 1 at Poughkeepsie, New York, show that the lodge was open for routine matters on the 26th of December, 1782; that it was closed until ten o'clock the next morning when Brother George Washington, Commander in Chief, Brothers Woolsey and Graham were announced as visitors. The minutes of the lodge continue as follows:

> "Lodge being closed till after Dinner. When the following Address was Presented to His Excellency, Bro. Washington: 'We the Master, Wardens and Brethren of Solomon's Lodge No. 1, are highly sensible of the Honor done to Masonry in general by the countenance shown to it by the most Dignified characters.' "

The records of Alexandria Lodge show that Washington was present on the 24th of June, 1784, when he was elected an honorary member of that lodge.

Washington was inaugurated President of the United States on the 30th of April, 1789, in New York City. Chancellor Robert R. Livingston of New York was Grand Master in the jurisdiction of New York at that time and the Chancellor administered to Washington the oath of office. The Bible used for this purpose was the Bible of St. Johns Lodge No. 1. It was secured by Major Jacob Morton who was Master of the lodge and who was one of the officials in charge of the inauguration procession. The Bible was brought by Major Morton from the lodge room to Federal Hall on what is now the corner of Broad and Wall Streets in the City of New York. It was opened at Genesis 49 where Washington laid his hand upon the verses from thirteen to thirty-three among which is Jacob's blessing of Joseph as the prince of his brethren. This Bible was printed in London by Mark Basket, printer to the King, in 1767. The story of Washington's oath taken upon this Bible is recorded on one of the fly-leaves.

It may be worth while to state parenthetically that the same Bible was used by Warren G. Harding when he took the oath of office as President on the 4th of March, 1921. The Bible is still the property of St. Johns Lodge, New York.

On the 18th of September, 1793, Washington laid the cornerstone of the national capitol. A bronze tablet marks the spot today. This tablet bears the following legend.

"Beneath this tablet the cornerstone of the Capitol of the United States was laid' by George Washington, First President, September 18, 1793."

There is a plate in the cornerstone reading as follows:

"This south-east corner-stone of the Capitol of the United States of America, in the city of Washington, was laid on the 18th day of September, 1793, in the thirteenth year of American Independence, in the first year of the second term of the presidency of George Washington, whose virtues in the civil administration of his country have been as conspicuous and beneficial as his military valor and prudence have been useful in establishing her liberties, and in the year of Masonry 5793, by the President of the United States, in concert with the Grand Lodge of Maryland, several Lodges under its jurisdiction and Lodge No. 22, from Alexandria, Virginia. Thomas Johnson, David Steuart, and Daniel Carroll, Commissioners. Joseph Clark, R.W.G.M. pro tem. James Hoban and Stephen Hallate, Architects. Collin Williamson, Master Mason."

The ceremonies in connection with the laying of the cornerstone were reported fully by the Columbian Mirror and Alexandria Gazette in its issue of September 25, 1793, and also in a Georgetown, D. C., paper of date September 21, 1793.

There was a military procession in which Washington marched. He laid the cornerstone of the capitol, deposited thereon the silver plate referred to a moment ago, and joined with those present in a prayer suitable to the occasion. Corn, wine and oil were then deposited upon the cornerstone, after which Masonic chanting honors were given.

Washington presented the gavel which was used on this occasion to Valentine Reintzel, Master of Lodge No. 9, Georgetown, District of Columbia. This lodge was afterwards known as Columbia Lodge No. 19 of Maryland. It suspended operations, but was re-organized as Potomac Lodge No. 43 under the authority of the Grand Lodge of Maryland. It subsequently became Potomac Lodge No. 5 under the authority of the Grand Lodge of the District of Columbia. This gavel was used on fifty-five occasions between 1793 and 1907. It has been used officially by the following Presidents: James K. Polk in laying the cornerstone of the Smithsonian Institution in 1847; Millard Fillmore at the extension to the United States capitol in 1851; James Buchanan at the dedication of Clark Mills' statue of Washington in 1860; William McKinley at the Washington Centennial exercises at Mount Vernon in 1899; Theodore Roosevelt at the Sesquicentennial celebration of Washington's initiation into Freemasonry held at Philadelphia in 1902; and Herbert Hoover at the cornerstone laying of the Department of Commerce Building in Washington.

The trowel and sash used by Washington at the laying of the corner-stone of the national capitol are now the property of the Alexandria Lodge above referred to. This lodge shortly after Washington's death changed its name to Alexandria Washington Lodge No. 22. The trowel was used when the cornerstone of the George Washington Masonic National Memorial was laid at Alexandria, November 1, 1923, the gavel being in the possession of President Coolidge and Chief Justice Taft upon that occasion. Silver replicas of it were used by all the visiting Grand Masters in attendance and were retained by them as mementos of the occasion.

There was a period in this country when Masonry was under a cloud. There was an anti-Masonic party in existence for many years and as late as 1880 it had a candidate for president. During this period of time an endeavor was made to raise a doubt as to Washington's interest in Masonry. Doubt was expressed as to whether he had in fact participated in Masonic services at the laying of the cornerstone of the national capitol. Benjamin B. French, Grand Master for the District of Columbia, in an address delivered at Mount Vernon on the 24th of June, 1851, discussed this subject. He states that he took the matter up by correspondence with George Washington Parke Custis, Martha Washington's grandson, and received from Mr. Custis a letter containing the following language:

> "There is not the shadow of a doubt but that Washington officiated as Grand Master of Masons of the United States in laying the cornerstone of the Capitol in 1793. He certainly wore the veritable apron now in possession of Alexandria Washington Lodge No. 22, and such other insignia as was suitable to his exalted rank as a Mason. The apron, &c., was given to the Lodge No. 22 by the executors of Washington, of whom I am the sole survivor."

The most interesting part of our subject has to do with Washington's Masonic correspondence. There are in existence fortunately a number of letters authentic beyond any doubt which give us in Washington's own words his attitude toward the Masonic institution.

The Revolutionary War closed in 1783. Early in December of that year Washington parted with the officers of the Continental Army at Fraunce's Tavern in New York. He surrendered his commission to Congress in session at Annapolis on the 23rd of December and reached Mount Vernon just in time for Christmas. Alexandria Lodge wrote him a fraternal letter of felicitation to which Washington replied as follows:

> "Mount Vernon, 28th Decr. 1783.
> Gentlemen:
>
> With pleasing sensibility I received your favor of the 26th, and beg leave to offer you my sincere thanks for the favorable sentiments with which it abounds.
>
> I shall always feel pleasure when it may be in my power to render service to Lodge No. 39, and in every act of brotherly kindness to the Members of it; being with great truth.
> Your affecte Brother and Obedt Servant
> G. Washington."

I have already spoken of the election of Washington as an honorary member of Alexandria Lodge on St. Johns Day, June 24, 1784. The invitation of the lodge to be present on that occasion was acknowledged by Washington in the following letter:

Mount Vernon, June 19, 1784.

Dear Sir:

With pleasure, I received the invitation of the master and members of Lodge No. 39, to dine with them on the approaching anniversary of St. John the Baptist. If nothing unforeseen at present interferes, I will have the honor of doing it. For the polite and flattering terms in which you have expressed their wishes, you will please accept my thanks.

With esteem and respect, I am, dear sir,
Your most Ob't serv't

G. Washington."

The State of Rhode Island did not ratify the Federal Constitution until May 29, 1790, more than a year after Washington became President. During this year Washington carefully refrained from visiting Rhode Island. He did however in August of 1790 make a visitation to the state and an address of welcome was prepared by King David's Lodge No. 1 of Newport, Rhode Island. Washington replied to this address on the 22nd of August, 1790, in the following language:

"To the Master, Wardens and Brethren of King Davids Lodge in Newport, Rhode Island.

Gentlemen,

I receive the welcome which you give me to Rhode Island with pleasure, and I acknowledge my obligations for the flattering expressions of regard, contained in your address, with grateful sincerity.

Being persuaded that a just application of the principles, on which the Masonic Fraternity is founded, must be promotive of private virtue and public prosperity, I shall always be happy to advance the interests of the Society, and to be considered by them as a deserving brother.

My best wishes, Gentlemen, are offered for your individual happiness.

G. Washington."

In 1791 Washington made a visitation of the southern states. He reached Georgetown, South Carolina, on the 30th of April, 1791. Here he was presented with an address by a committee from Prince George's Lodge No. 16. Washington replied to this address as follows:

"To the Brethren of Prince George's Lodge, No. 16.
Gentlemen:

The cordial welcome which you give me to George-town, and the congratulations, you are pleased to offer on my election to the chief magistracy receive my grate-ful thanks.

I am much obliged by your good wishes and re-ciprocate them with sincerity assuring the fraternity of my esteem, I request them to believe that I shall always be ambitious of being considered a deserving Brother.

G. Washington."

When Washington made this trip through the southern states General Mordecai Gist was Grand Master in the jurisdiction of South Carolina. Gist was a native of Baltimore and had commanded Maryland troops in the Revolutionary War. He fought with great gallantry under Washington at the Battle of Long Island and in the latter part of the war was one of the most efficient officers in the army of the south. When Washington came into Gist's Masonic jurisdiction in 1791 General Gist wrote him a letter, the original of which is now in the possession of the Iowa Masonic Library at Cedar Rapids. The letter is too long for quotation in full in this paper. It is in part as follows:

"To the President of the United States.
Sir:

Induc'd by respect for your public and private character as well as the relation in which you stand with the Brethren of this Society, We The Grand Lodge of the State of South Carolina, Ancient York Masons beg leave to offer our sincere congratulations on your arrival in this state. * * *

Distinguish'd always by your virtues more than the exalted stations, in which you have mov'd, we exult in the opportunity you now give us of hailing you Brother of our Order; and trust from your knowledge of our Institution to meet your countenance and support.

With fervent zeal for your happiness, we pray that a life so dear to the bosom of this Society and to mankind in general, may be long, very long preserv'd; and when you leave the temporal Symbolic Lodges of this world, you may be receiv'd into that Celestial Lodge of Perfection where the Grand Master Architect of the Universe presides.

Done in behalf of the Grand Lodge.

M. Gist, G.M."

Charleston 2d May, 1791."

Washington's reply to this letter is as follows:

"Gentlemen:—I am much obliged by the respect which you are so good as to declare for my public and private character. I recognize with pleasure my relation to the brethren of your Society, and I accept with gratitude your congratulations on my arrival in South Carolina.

Your sentiments, on the establishment and exercise of our equal government, are worthy of an association, whose principles lead to purity of morals, and are beneficial of action.

The fabric of our freedom is placed on the enduring basis of public virtue, and will, I fondly hope, long continue to protect the prosperity of the architects who raised it. I shall be happy, on every occasion, to evince my regard for the Fraternity. For your prosperity individually, I offer my best wishes.

G. Washington."

In 1792 the Grand Lodge of Massachusetts printed a volume entitled "Constitutions of the Honorable Fraternity of Free and Accepted Masons." It was dedicated to Washington in the following language:

"In Testimony of His Exalted Merit, and of Our Inalienable Regard, This Work Is Inscribed and Dedicated to our Illustrious Brother George Washington: The Friend of Masonry, of his Country, and of Man."

A copy of the book was presented to Washington. This book is now in the Washington collection of the Boston Atheneum. It is beautifully bound in tree calf. It bears the signature of G. Washington in the upper right hand corner of the title page. The facts with reference to the presentation are contained in the minutes of the Grand Lodge of Massachusetts under date of March 11, 1793. Washington's reply to the letter of presentation is as follows:

> "To the Grand Lodge of Free & Accepted Masons, for the Commonwealth of Massachusetts.
>
> Flattering as it may be to the human mind, & truly honorable as it is to receive from our fellow citizens testimonies of approbation for exertions to promote the public welfare, it is not less pleasing to know, that the milder virtues of the heart are highly respected by a Society whose liberal principles must be founded in the immutable laws of truth and justice.
>
> To enlarge the sphere of social happiness is worthy the benevolent design of a masonic institution; and it is most fervently to be wished, that the conduct of every member of the fraternity, as well as those publications that discover the principles which actuate them; may tend to convince mankind that the grand object of Masonry is to promote the happiness of the human race.
>
> While I beg your acceptance of my thanks for the 'Book of Constitutions' which you have sent me, & the honor you have done me in the dedication, permit me to assure you that I feel all those emotions of gratitude which your affectionate address & cordial wishes are calculated to inspire; and I sincerely pray that the Great Architect of the Universe may bless you here, and receive you hereafter into his immortal Temple.
>
> G. Washington.."

Several months following the farewell message of Washington the Grand Lodge of Pennsylvania addressed a letter to him which letter was delivered in person on the 28th of December, 1796. Washington replied to this address in a letter penned by his own hand. This letter is as follows:

> "Fellow-Citizens and Brothers, of the Grand Lodge of Pennsylvania.
>
> I have received your address with all the feelings of brotherly affection, mingled with those sentiments, for the Society, which it was calculated to excite.
>
> To have been, in any degree, an instrument in the hands of Providence, to promote order and union, and erect upon a solid foundation the true principles of government, is only to have shared with many others in a labour, the result of which let us hope, will prove through all ages, a sanctuary for brothers and a lodge for the virtues.—

> Permit me to reciprocate your prayers for my temporal happiness, and to supplicate that we may all meet thereafter in that eternal temple, whose builder is the great Architect of the Universe.
>
> G. Washington."

When Washington retired from the Presidency and resumed his residence at Mount Vernon in March, 1797, a formal letter of felicitation was sent him by Alexandria Lodge No. 22. He attended the meeting of the Lodge held on the 1st of April, 1797, and his reply to the letter of felicitation sent him by the lodge was read at that time. It is as follows:

> "Brothers of the Ancient York Masons of Lodge No. 22.
>
> While my heart acknowledges with Brotherly Love, your affectionate congratulations on my retirement from the arduous toils of past years, my gratitude is no less excited by your kind wishes for my future happiness.—
>
> If it has pleased the Supreme Architect of the Universe to make me an humble instrument to promote the welfare and happiness of my fellow men, my exertions have been abundantly recompensed by the kind partiality with which they have been received; and the assurance you give me of your belief that I have acted upon the square in my public capacity, will be among my principal enjoyments in this Terrestrial Lodge.
>
> G. Washington."

Two Masonic aprons which were undoubtedly used by Washington are still in existence. One of them, presented by Messrs. Watson and Cassoul of Nantes, France, is in the possession of Alexandria Washington Lodge, and the other embroidered by the Marquise de Lafayette and presented to Washington by her husband in August, 1784, is now in the possession of the Grand Lodge of Pennsylvania.

Washington died on the 14th of December, 1799. On Monday, December 16, his funeral was conducted with Masonic ceremonies. Fifty-six members of Alexandria Lodge, fifteen of Brook Lodge and a delegation from Federal City Lodge participated in the funeral. All of the pallbearers were Masons and with one exception all of them were members of Alexandria Lodge. Rev. Thomas Davis, rector of Christ Church, Alexandria, officiated at the funeral, and the Masonic services held in connection therewith were conducted by Dr. Elisha Cullen Dick, Master of Alexandria Lodge, aided by Rev. James Muir, its chaplain.

There are other Masonic letters of Washington of undoubted authenticity, but it would unduly prolong this paper to quote them. There is besides a large amount of tradition and suggestion with reference to Washington's Masonic career which it is unnecessary to notice. The facts already recited are sufficient for our purposes. Two concluding observations are pertinent.

There is no discounting the Masonic loyalty of the author of these letters. Joseph Dillaway Sawyer in his recent and scholarly life of Washington devotes considerable space to Washington's Masonic career. He uses the following language in which I heartily concur:

> "When, in the full promise of his splendid youth,—being not yet twenty-one,—George Washington entered the little lodge room in Fredericksburg for initiation into the Masonic Order, he followed a light which has guided mankind for uncounted centuries; for the esoteric beginning of the order is so ancient that its true origin is hidden in the mists of antiquity. The beautiful symbolism of the Order must have appealed to Washington's youthful imagination as fervently as the ritual appealed to the devotional side of his nature. It is at least certain that, with the earnestness and thoroughness that distinguished his actions in every walk of life, Washington entered into the full spirit of the Order, carrying its mystical light with him into all of his enterprises. Any sincere and earnest Mason, closely scanning Washington's writings and public speeches, would immediately recognize the author of them as one of the brotherhood, for many of his expressions are rich in Masonic meaning. Washington was a Mason in every fibre of his being; he thought Masonry, practiced Masonry, lived Masonry, in every important act of his life."

Let us also note that Washington was initiated as an Entered Apprentice before his twenty-first birthday. He was passed and raised in his twenty-second year. He was a Mason when he won his spurs on the fateful day of Braddock's defeat. He was a Mason when beneath the elm at Cambridge he took command of the Revolutionary army. He was a Mason on Christmas night 1776 when he crossed the Delaware amid the floating ice to surprise and capture the drunken Hessians and restore the cause which the faint-hearted had given up as lost. He was a Mason when he rode the hills about Valley Forge, keeping the army together by his matchless personality and his unshaken faith. He was a Mason when he effected the junction on the banks of York River of the French and American forces which overwhelmed Cornwallis and won from Great Britain her recognition of American independence. He was a Mason when he presided over the Constitutional Convention. He was a Mason when as our first president he transformed the insolvency of the critical period into the prosperity of government under the Constitution. He was a Mason on the 17th of September, 1796, when, his great work well nigh done, he gave to the country in his Farewell Address the chart by which the Ship of State has been navigated for thirteen decades.

At every step of his marvelously fruitful life the way was illumined by the light which shines at the altar of Masonry. When he passed away our institution lost its most eminent member and the world lost its first gentleman.

The following mystical pictures are not related to this book.

They have been included for your enjoyment.

Pictures 1

Pictures 2

FAITH, HOPE, AND CHARITY.

Pictures 3

Pictures 4

Pictures 5

ALCHYMIA
(From Thurneysser's Quinta Essentia, 1570)

Pictures 7

Pictures 8

Pictures 9

Assyrian Type of Gilgamesh

Pictures 11

MASONIC APRON PRESENTED TO GEN. WASHINGTON
BY MADAME LAFAYETTE.

Pictures 13

THE GOLDEN WHEEL

Pictures 15

Pictures 16

Pictures 17

Pictures 18

Pictures 19

Pictures 20

Pictures 21

Pictures 22

Pictures 23

Pictures 24

Pictures 25

MERCURIUS DE MERCURIO

Pictures 26

Pictures 27

Pictures 28

Pictures 29

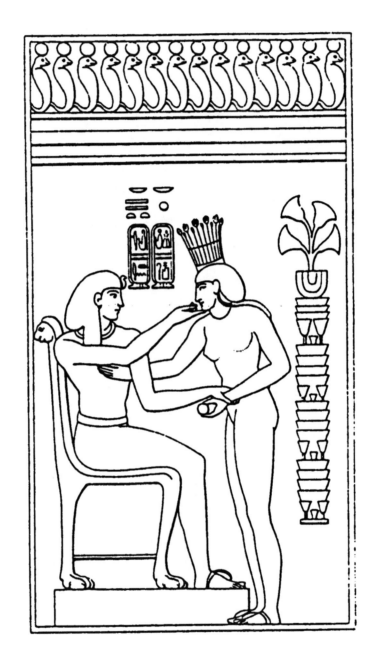

Pictures 30

Pictures 31

Pictures 32

Pictures 33

Pictures 34

Pictures 35

Pictures 36

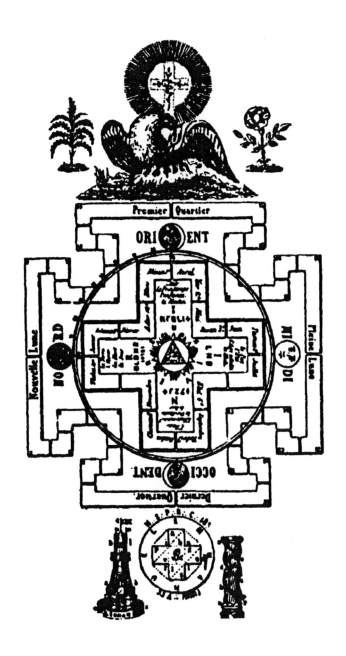

Pictures 37

Pictures 38

Pictures 39

Pictures 40

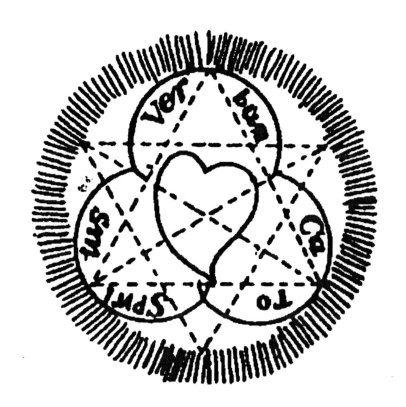

Pictures 41

Pictures 42

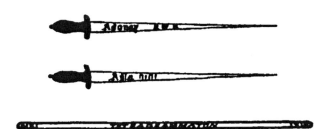

THE MAGIC CIRCLE AND WEAPONS.

Pictures 43

Pictures 44

Pictures 45

Pictures 46

Pictures 47

Pictures 48

Pictures 49

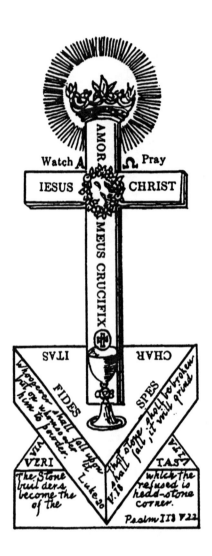

Pictures 50

Pictures 51

Pictures 52

Pictures 53

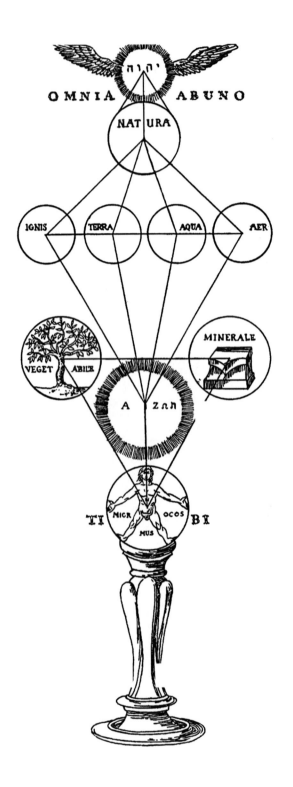

Pictures 54

Pictures 55

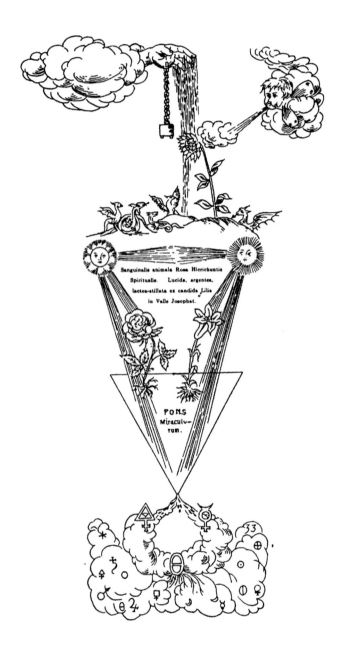

Pictures 56

Pictures 57

Pictures 58

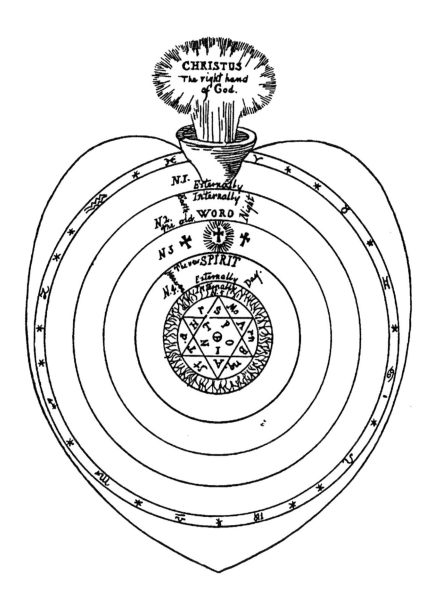

Pictures 59

Pictures 60

Pictures 61

Spiritus, Anima, Corpus.

Pictures 63

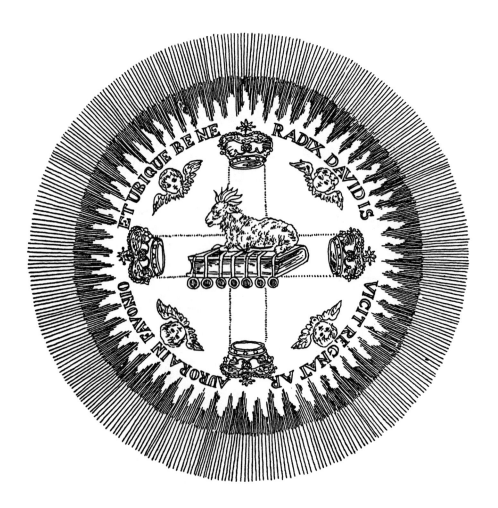

Pictures 64

Pictures 65

Pictures 66

Pictures 67

THE GOLDEN WHEEL

Pictures 69

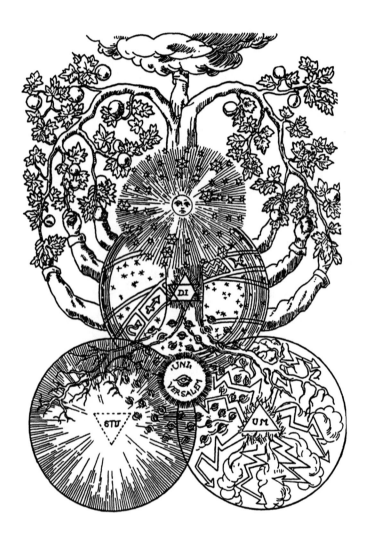

Pictures 70

Pictures 71

Pictures 72

Pictures 73

Pictures 74

Pictures 75

Apocalyptic Key

Pictures 77

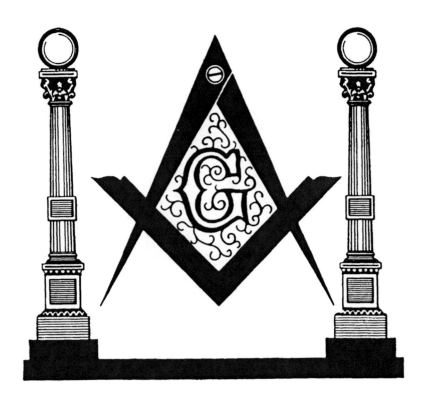

Pictures 78

Pictures 79

Pictures 80

Pictures 81

Pictures 82

Pictures 83

Pictures 84

Pictures 85

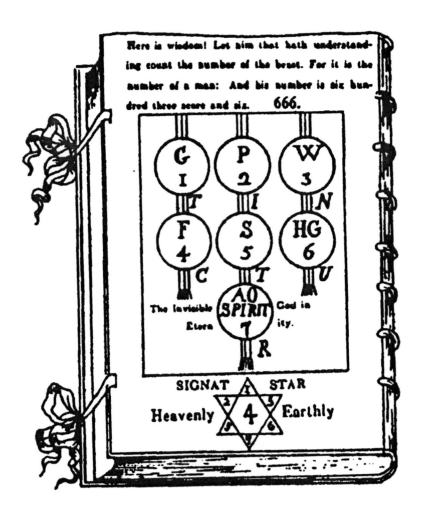

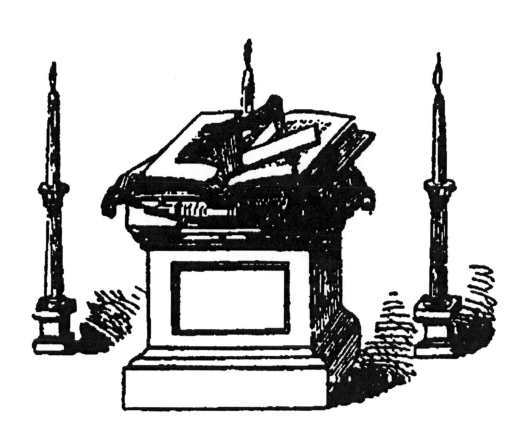

Pictures 87

Pictures 88

Breinigsville, PA USA
08 November 2009
227215BV00001B/29/A